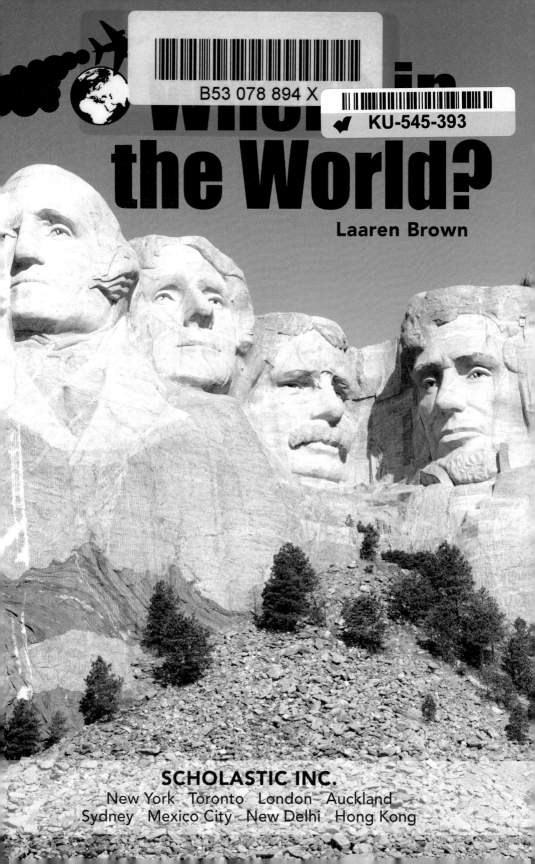

Where in the World?

Laaren Brown

SCHOLASTIC INC.

New York   Toronto   London   Auckland
Sydney   Mexico City   New Delhi   Hong Kong

Read more! Do more!

After you read this book, download your free all-new digital activities.

You can show what a great reader you are!

discover more readers

Where in the World?

reading fun

enter

For Mac and PC

True or false?

see draw home

Where in the World? true or false?

Where in the World? true or false?

Where in the World? true or false?

true false

true false

true

Play games and do activities with videos and sounds!

Make a landmarks map

Stick famous landmarks on a map of the world. Include the ones in your book. Find out about others, too!

back home

You will need . . .

A pencil

Thin card

Crayons, markers, or paints and a paintbrush

Scissors Tape or glue

Now click the numbers . . .

1 2 3

Log on to
**www.scholastic.com/
discovermore/readers**
Enter this special code:
L3P29TGPD453

Contents

4 Where in the world?

6 The Americas

14 Europe

20 Where else in the world?

28 Where to next?

30 Glossary

32 Index

Distributed in the UK by Scholastic UK Ltd, Westfield Road, Southam, Warwickshire, England CV47 0RA

ISBN 978-1-407-14246-3

12 11 10 9 8 7 6 5 4 3 2 1   14 15 16 17 18 19/0

Printed in the USA 40
First published 2014

Scholastic is constantly working to lessen the environmental impact of our manufacturing processes. To view our industry-leading paper procurement policy, visit www.scholastic.com/paperpolicy.

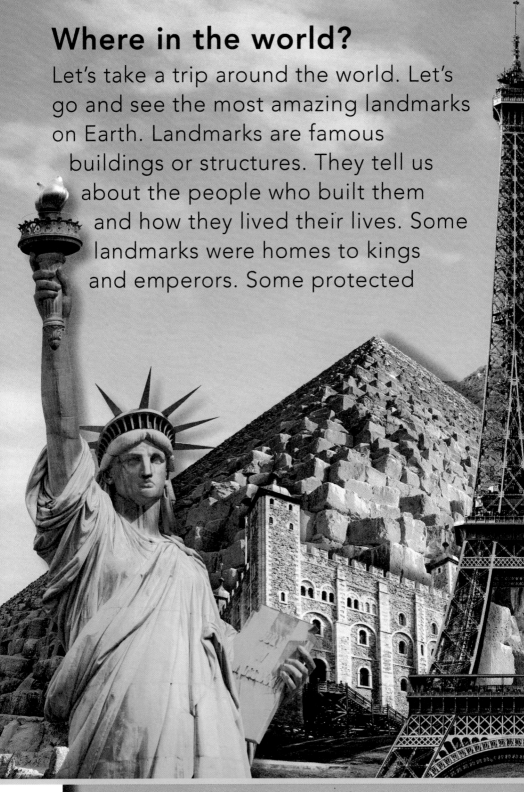

Where in the world?

Let's take a trip around the world. Let's go and see the most amazing landmarks on Earth. Landmarks are famous buildings or structures. They tell us about the people who built them and how they lived their lives. Some landmarks were homes to kings and emperors. Some protected

THINK ABOUT IT **If you could go anywhere**

their countries from enemies. Some were built to remember important people who had died. Landmarks tell us about what was important to the people who built them. They tell us what those people valued most. They make the people in their countries proud.

NEW WORD

Many tourists visit a country's **landmarks** (LAND-mahrks).

SAY IT OUT LOUD

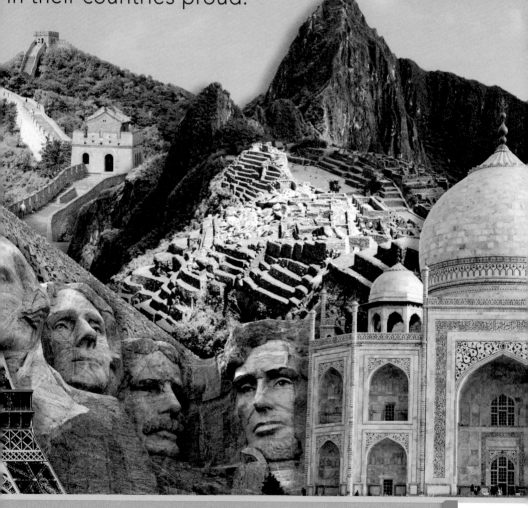

n the world, where would you go?

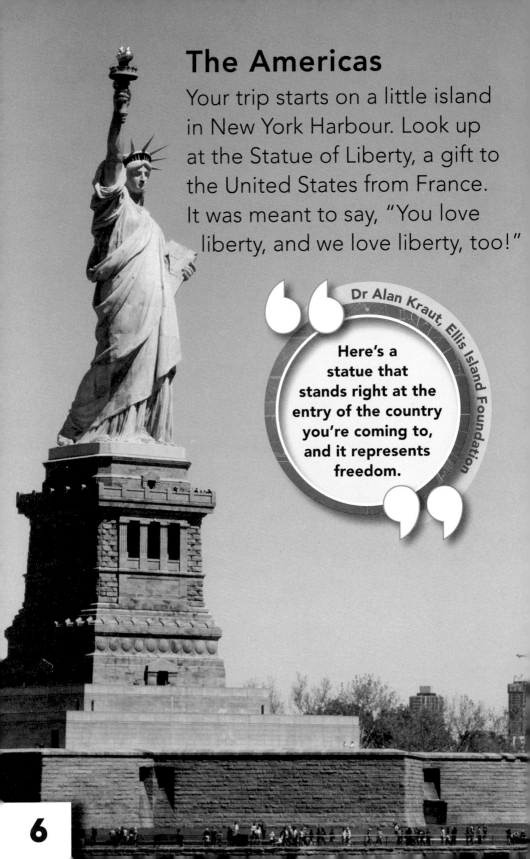

The Americas

Your trip starts on a little island in New York Harbour. Look up at the Statue of Liberty, a gift to the United States from France. It was meant to say, "You love liberty, and we love liberty, too!"

Dr Alan Kraut, Ellis Island Foundation

Here's a statue that stands right at the entry of the country you're coming to, and it represents freedom.

The lady with the torch lights the way to Ellis Island. For more than 30 years, people from all around the world entered the United States there. The statue is a symbol of the USA, the land of the free.

Come on in!

Between 1851 and 1910, about 25 million people entered the USA, at Ellis Island and other places.

NEW WORD

People who have **liberty** (LIB-ur-tee) are free to do what they want.

SAY IT OUT LOUD

2,598,000	2,315,000	2,812,000	5,147,000	3,688,000	8,795,000
1851–1860	1861–1870	1871–1880	1881–1890	1891–1900	1901–1910

Travel west 2,776 km (1,725 miles) and you'll arrive at Mount Rushmore in the Black Hills of South Dakota. In 1927, work began on a grand project there. Sculptor Gutzon Borglum organized 400 workers.

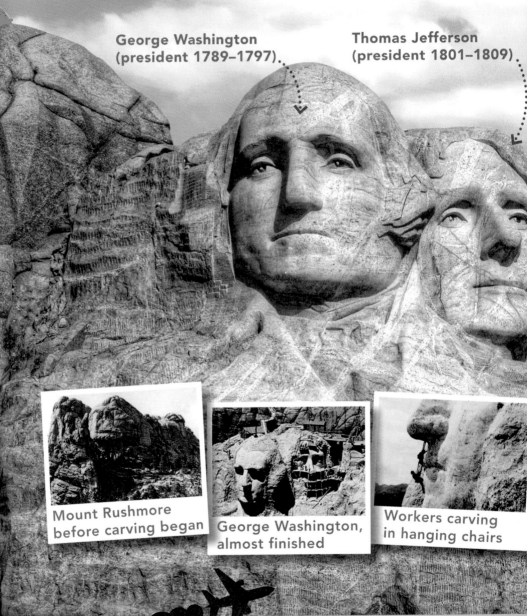

George Washington (president 1789–1797).

Thomas Jefferson (president 1801–1809).

Mount Rushmore before carving began

George Washington, almost finished

Workers carving in hanging chairs

Work on a secret cave room

They blasted away tonnes of rock with dynamite, then carved giant faces. Today, four US presidents stare out from the rock. What made these four so special? They all had big ideas for the USA, and they made those ideas come to life. Mount Rushmore inspires Americans to work together to make the USA great.

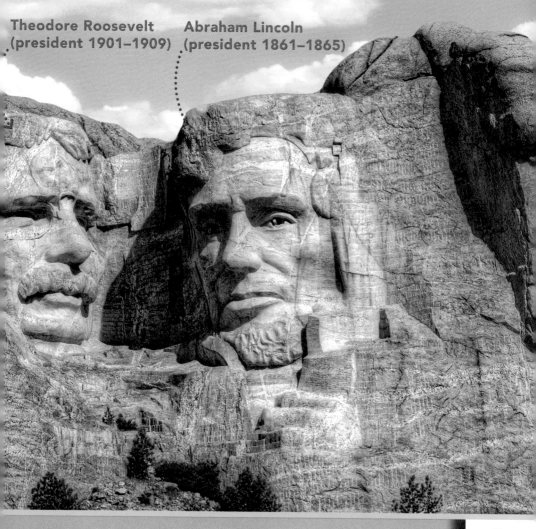

Theodore Roosevelt
(president 1901–1909)

Abraham Lincoln
(president 1861–1865)

ehind the faces was started but never finished.

Moving west over the Rocky Mountains, you'll find the huge and awe-inspiring Hoover Dam. Not only is it beautiful, but it works hard, too! The dam helps control the flow of the Colorado River. It uses the flow to make electricity. It produces all the energy needed by 1.3 million people in California, Nevada, and Arizona.

Water flows into towers.

Hoover Dam

Hoover Dam

Water is piped into turbines.

Colorado River

Building the dam in the 1930s was a massive effort. Many people said it couldn't be done! But Herbert Hoover, the 31st president, backed the project and work started on the dam. It is one of the largest structures in the world and is visited by more than 1 million people a year.

INSIDE A TURBINE

Wires carry the electricity to towns and cities...

Water makes the turbines spin. That produces electricity.

Now take a trip to Peru, in South America. You can climb so high, it feels like you're touching the Sun! At Machu Picchu, in the Andes Mountains, lie the ruins of an amazing palace. The palace was full of life 600 years ago. It was built for an emperor so that he could be close to the Sun.

To the Inca people, the emperor wasn't just a ruler. He was a god. So he needed a place to relax that was like the home of the gods.

TIMELINE

1450
The Inca emperor ordered his workers to build Machu Picchu.

1455–1530
Inca emperors used Machu Picchu as a summer palace.

1524–1526
Two-thirds of the Inca people died from a disease.

1532
Spanish soldiers invaded Peru, searching for gold. They made the Incas slaves.

1530s
Machu Picchu was abandoned. The Spanish never found the palace.

1911
American Hiram Bingham discovered the ruins of Machu Picchu.

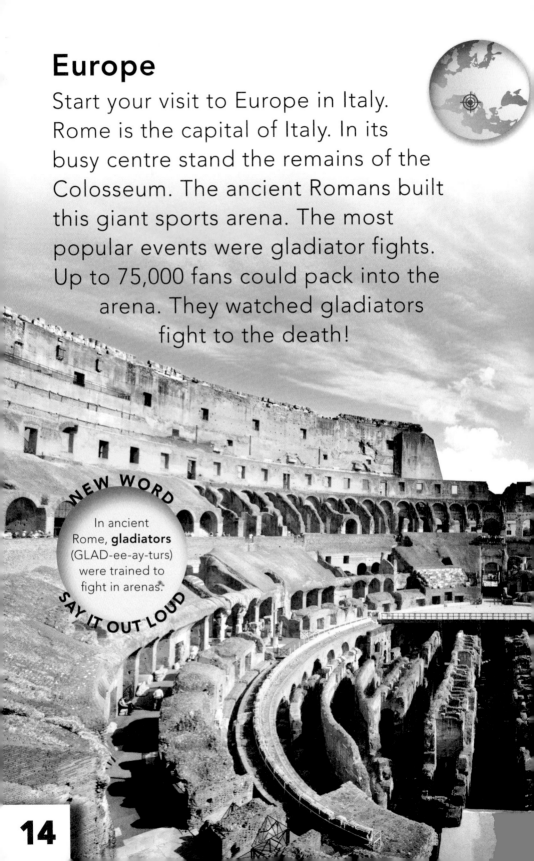

Europe

Start your visit to Europe in Italy. Rome is the capital of Italy. In its busy centre stand the remains of the Colosseum. The ancient Romans built this giant sports arena. The most popular events were gladiator fights. Up to 75,000 fans could pack into the arena. They watched gladiators fight to the death!

NEW WORD

In ancient Rome, **gladiators** (GLAD-ee-ay-turs) were trained to fight in arenas.

SAY IT OUT LOUD

Parthenon

Travel east to Greece. The Parthenon is one of the most beautiful ancient buildings of all. The ancient Greeks built it for Athena, their goddess of wisdom.

GLADIATOR FIGHTS

Weapons

Gladiators learned to fight in special schools. Then they usually fought to the death.

Trident

Dagger

Net

Battles

Sometimes gladiators had big battles. They fought one another from chariots drawn by horses.

Wild animals

Lions and tigers were kept in pens under the arena. They were brought up to fight the gladiators.

Make sure to stop in London, the capital city of England. Towering over the River Thames is a mighty castle. A king built the Tower of London in about 1100 to show his power. Later, part of it became a dark and terrible prison. Many important people were kept there.

DEATHS AT THE TOWER

Anne Boleyn

One of the six wives of King Henry VIII, Anne was beheaded in 1536.

Catherine Howard

Catherine was another o Henry VIII's wives! He had her beheaded in 154

Some were tortured. Some were put to death. Today, the tower is guarded by special soldiers called Beefeaters. Six ravens also live there. It is said that if the number of ravens drops below six, the tower – and England – will fall.

Lady Jane Grey
Queen of England for only nine days, she was beheaded in 1554.

Robert Devereux
He led an army against Queen Elizabeth I. He was beheaded in 1601.

Imagine this! You're in Paris, France, and it's 31 March 1889. You're going to be the first person to climb the Eiffel Tower! The lifts aren't ready yet. So Gustave Eiffel, the tower's designer, leads you up the stairs. You climb and climb . . . until at last you stand 276 metres (906 feet) above Paris. Soon the French flag is snapping in the breeze. You watch a happy crowd celebrate far below. The tallest landmark in Paris is open!

EIFFEL TOWER BY THE NUMBERS

August 1887

March 1888

September 1888

Number of rivets:
2,500,000
Number of metal
parts: 18,000

Number of
lifts: 7,
travelling
103,000 km
(64,000 miles)
per year

Number of
steps to the
top: 1,665

Where else in the world?

You are standing on hot desert sand near Cairo, in Egypt. Raise your eyes. You will see an enormous pyramid soaring above you. The Great Pyramid is the only remaining Wonder of the Ancient World. It was built about 4,600 years ago. It was a tomb for a king named Khufu.

Each side is 230 m. (755 ft) long.

INSIDE THE GREAT PYRAMID

Khufu's burial chamber

Air shaft

Underground room

When it was first built, the

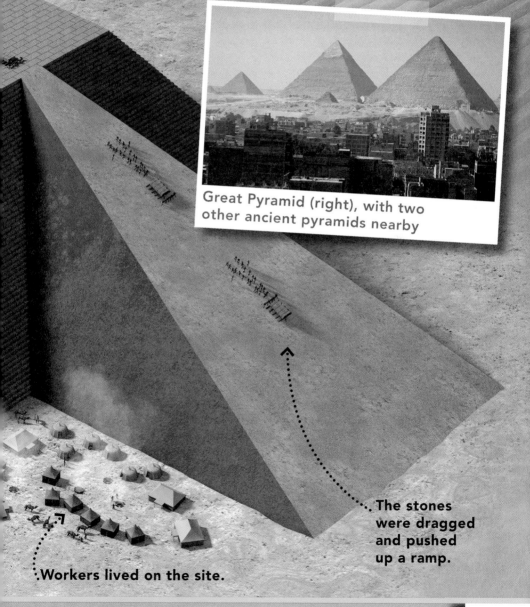

The Great Pyramid is made of 2.3 million blocks of heavy stone. It was the tallest building in the world for nearly 4,000 years.

Great Pyramid (right), with two other ancient pyramids nearby

The stones were dragged and pushed up a ramp.

Workers lived on the site.

Thousands of kilometres to the east, you will reach the Great Wall of China. This is the longest structure on Earth. The first emperor of China built it to protect his empire. When you stand on it, you can imagine that you are a Chinese soldier keeping a lookout.

The widest section of the wall is 9 m (30 ft). It is said that one worker died for every 0.3 m (1 ft) of its length. Today, some sections are in ruins.

In 2012, Chinese experts showed that the Great Wall is 21,195 km (13,170 miles) long. That's more than twice as long as people once thought it was!

Stretched out, the wall would reach halfway around the world.

It's four times as long as the United States is wide.

It's as long as 2,395 Mount Everests, stacked on top of one another, are tall.

It's the same length as 7,728,366 people holding hands . . .

. . . or 662,412 blue whales, nose to tail.

Once upon a time, there was an emperor in northern India who loved his wife very much. But she died. The emperor was so sad that he built a beautiful marble tomb, the Taj Mahal. From the outside, everyone could see the gleaming dome. Four minarets stood at the four corners. Inside, it was decorated with rich and colourful gems.

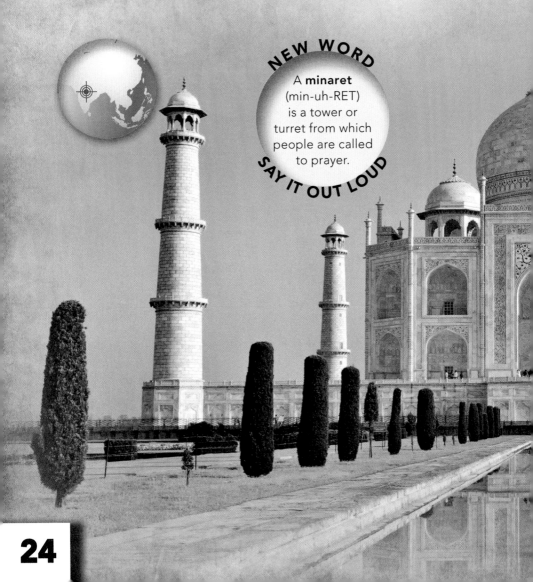

NEW WORD

A **minaret** (min-uh-RET) is a tower or turret from which people are called to prayer.

SAY IT OUT LOUD

This is the true love story of Shah Jahan and his beloved wife Mumtaz Mahal. She died in 1631. It took 22,000 workers 22 years to build her magnificent tomb in the city of Agra. When the shah died in 1666, his body was placed inside, alongside his wife's. The Taj Mahal reminds us to think of those we love and those we have lost.

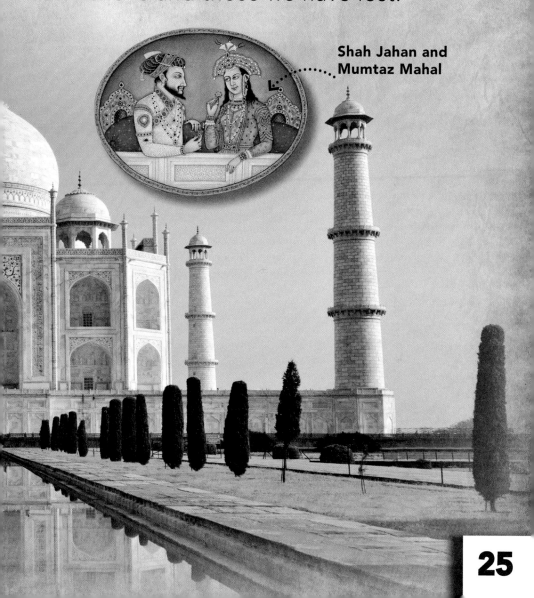

Shah Jahan and Mumtaz Mahal

Your world tour ends in another harbour. This one is in Australia. You are on the other side of the world from New York, where you started. What do you think of the Sydney Opera House? Does it look like a sailing ship to you? Or like the wings of a bird?

There are over 1 million tiles on the roof. Each section of roof weighs up to 13.5 tonnes. The bridge, hundreds of boats, and the glittering water are spread out before you. It's one of the most beautiful sights in the world. It's a great place to end your journey.

Where to next?

Montreal Biosphere

Visitors flock to this science museum in Canada. They can walk around its giant dome. It is 76 m (249 ft) wide and 62 m (203 ft) high!

McMurdo Station

This is a US research station in Antarctica. More than 1,000 people live and work there. It is the largest "town" in Antarctica.

Robben Island

The jail on this island off South Africa is famous. This is because of one prisoner – the freedom fighter Nelson Mandela. He was freed in 1990 after 27 years.

Nelson Mandela

THINK ABOUT IT **Why are the landmarks o**

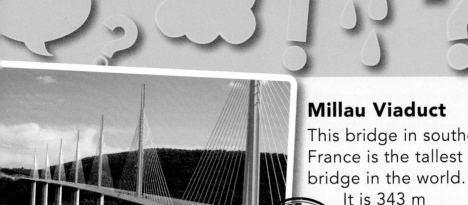

Millau Viaduct

This bridge in southern France is the tallest bridge in the world. It is 343 m (1,125 ft) high! It crosses the valley of the River Tarn.

United Nations Headquarters

The United Nations (UN) was formed in 1945. It aims to keep peace between all countries. Its building is in New York City. More than 1 million people visit it each year.

Burj Khalifa

This skyscraper in Dubai is the tallest man-made structure in the world. It is 828 m (2,717 ft) from the ground to the top.

nese pages important to people?

Glossary

abandon
To leave something behind and never go back.

ancient
Very old, or from long ago.

arena
A large area or building used for sports and fun.

Beefeater
A special soldier who guards the Tower of London.

behead
To kill someone by cutting off his or her head.

chariot
A small vehicle with two wheels, pulled by horses.

dam
A barrier built across a river to control its flow.

disease
A sickness that spreads from person to person.

dome
A large round roof.

dynamite
A material that explodes, used to blast rock apart.

electricity
A type of energy that powers lights and machines.

emperor
The male ruler of an empire, or kingdom.

gladiator
A person trained to fight in arenas in ancient Rome.

harbour
An area of water near land, where boats can stop safely.

Inca
A member of a South American Indian people who lived in Peru from about 1100 to the early 1530s.

landmark
A building or structure that is very important to people.

liberty
Freedom.

minaret
A tower or turret from which people are called to prayer.

pyramid
A tomb built by ancient Egyptians. A pyramid has sides shaped like triangles.

ramp
A sloping surface that joins two surfaces at different levels.

raven
A type of large black bird.

rivet
A metal pin that holds two pieces of metal together.

sculptor
A person who makes art by carving or shaping stone, wood, or metal.

slave
A person who is owned by another person.

tomb
A building or room for holding a dead body.

turbine
A machine with blades that are moved by water, wind, or gas.

viaduct
A bridge that carries a road or railroad over a valley.

Index

A
Agra 25
Americas 6–13
Andes Mountains 12
Antarctica 28
Arizona 10
Athena 15
Australia 26

B
battles 15
Beefeaters 17
beheadings 16–17
Bingham, Hiram 13
Black Hills, South Dakota 8–9
Boleyn, Anne 16
Borglum, Gutzon 8
bridge 29
Burj Khalifa 29

C
Cairo 20
California 10
Canada 28
castle 16–17
Colorado River 10–11
Colosseum 14–15

D
Devereux, Robert 17
Dubai 29
dynamite 9

E
Egypt 20–21
Eiffel, Gustave 18
Eiffel Tower 18–19
electricity 10, 11
Elizabeth I 17
Ellis Island 7
England 16–17
Europe 14–19

F
France 6, 18–19, 29

G
gladiators 14–15
gold 13
Great Pyramid 20–21
Great Wall of China 22–23
Greece 15
Grey, Lady Jane 17

H
Henry VIII 16
Hoover Dam 10–11
Hoover, Herbert 11
Howard, Catherine 16

I
Inca people 12, 13
India 24–25
Italy 14

J
Jefferson, Thomas 8

K
Khufu 20
Kraut, Alan 6

L
Lifts 18, 19
Lincoln, Abraham 9
lions 15
London 16–17

M
Machu Picchu 12–13
Mandela, Nelson 28
McMurdo Station 28
Millau Viaduct 29
Montreal Biosphere 28
Mount Rushmore 8–9
Mumtaz Mahal 24–25

N O
Nevada 10
New York City 26, 29
New York Harbour 6–7

P Q
Paris 18–19
Parthenon 15
Peru 12–13
prison 16–17
pyramids 20–21

R
ravens 17
River Tarn 29
River Thames 16–17

Robben Island 28
Rocky Mountains 10
Romans 14, 15
Rome 14, 15
Roosevelt, Theodore 9

S
Shah Jahan 24–25
slaves 13
soldiers 13, 17, 22
South Africa 28
Spanish 13
Statue of Liberty 6
Sun 12
Sydney Opera House 26–27

T
Taj Mahal 24–25
tigers 15
tomb 20–21, 24–25
Tower of London 16–17
turbines 11

U V
United Nations 29
United States 6–11

W X Y Z
Washington, George 8
weapons 15